1 9 8 7

Cardinals in the Ice Age

THE NATIONAL POETRY SERIES

CARDINALS
IN THE
ICE AGE

POEMS BY

John Engels

[signature: John Engels]

 GRAYWOLF PRESS · SAINT PAUL

ACKNOWLEDGMENTS

Some of the poems in this collection first appeared in the following journals:
Antaeus: 'Dead Dog'; *Back Door*: 'Flicker'; *Bennington Review*: 'The Marshes';
Black Warrior Review: 'Apple Trees' (This poem also appeared in *The Seasons
in Vermont*, published by Tamarack Editions, Syracuse, New York, 1981.);
The Bread Loaf Anthology of Contemporary American Poetry: 'Revisit,' 'Or-
chard,' 'Goldfinch,' 'Cardinals in the Ice Age'; *Kenyon Review*: 'Cobra,' 'The
Raft'; *Massachusetts Review:* 'The Ash Grove in October'; *New England Review
& Bread Loaf Quarterly*: 'Winter Flight,' 'The Silence,' 'Patterns of Sleep,'
'Snowy Owl' and 'Night Flight in Ljubljana' ('Winter Flight' won a Push-
cart Prize in 1983, as well as the narrative poetry prize awarded annually by
New England Review & Bread Loaf Quarterly.); *The New Yorker*: 'Cardinals'
(Copyright 1981 *The New Yorker*); *North by Northeast*: 'Sunrise'; *Southern Hu-
manities Review*: 'Photograph,' 'Avocados'; *The Texas Review*: 'A Watercolor,'
'The Planet.'

I am grateful to the National Endowment for the Arts and to the Faculty
Council of St. Michael's College for support during the completion of this
collection. I also appreciate the opportunity to have traveled in Yugoslavia
under the provisions of the Fulbright Award. My special thanks go to
Georgene Lovecky, of the Commission for the International Exchange of
Scholars, and to Ivan Gadjansky, executive director of the Yugoslavian-
American Commission for Educational Exchange.   —JOHN ENGELS

Publication of this volume is made possible in part by a grant from the National Endowment for the Arts, and in part by generous contributions to
Graywolf Press from individuals, corporations and foundations.

ISBN 0-915308-91-6
Library of Congress Catalog Card Number 86-80012
First Printing, 1987
9 8 7 6 5 4 3 2
Published by GRAYWOLF PRESS
Post Office Box 75006, Saint Paul
Minnesota 55175

THE NATIONAL POETRY SERIES

The National Poetry Series was established in 1978 to publish five collections of poetry annually through five participating publishers. The manuscripts are selected by five poets of national reputation. Publication is funded by James A. Michener, Edward J. Piszek, The Copernicus Society, The Mobil Foundation, The National Endowment for the Arts, The Friends of the National Poetry Series and the five publishers—E. P. Dutton, Graywolf Press, William Morrow & Co., Persea Books and the University of Illinois Press.

1986

LITTLE STAR
Mark Halliday
Selected by Heather McHugh / William Morrow & Co.

CITIES IN MOTION
Sylvia Moss
Selected by Derek Walcott / University of Illinois Press

JUNK CITY
Barbara Anderson
Selected by Robert Pinsky / Persea Books

CARDINALS IN THE ICE AGE
John Engels
Selected by Philip Levine / Graywolf Press

RED ROADS
Charlie Smith
Selected by Stanley Kunitz / E. P. Dutton

TABLE OF CONTENTS

To VINCENT ENGELS,

*companion on the stream, intimate to the ways
of trouts and salmons, prophet of* E. Subvaria,
*bookman, poet, journalist, historian,
uncle, father, and extraordinary
friend of a lifetime:*

this book, with love

A WATERCOLOR

The paper was too wet – the colors ran.
Greens went olive; blues turned flat
in ways I'd not intended. Blacks and browns
bloomed in little soft rosettes

which bled into the lesser densities of hue;
for lofty in the hierarchies of my error
there stood great readiness to let
water do the work; nor had I learned

to love transparency, nor yet
to hold the paper's whiteness
in correct regard – therefore
such failed renderings: dull trees around

a cloudy pond. I turned away the better to see out
over the field to where the woods should be.
The woods were night-ridden, though a voice
rose at the field's farther edge,

something like a rush of leaves.
It was too dark to see, but when I turned
the air shone for a second where my hand
had rested, then transformed itself

into a membrane of green fire that traced
my moving arm . . . so for a time
I paced, gesturing about the room
to see complexly flare and fail the light

– though soon enough I tired
and came again to the window, wanting air.

3

CARDINALS IN THE ICE AGE

Apple Trees

Among the cherry saplings in the spring
I see the lichenous dry trunk
of the wild Spy, its one-limbed

blossoming. Then, in fall,
the McIntosh turns black of leaf
after one thin bearing of a dozen fruits,

and I am obliged to fell it. But in May
it springs up hairy in a vigor of new shoots,
and I cut them back, and they

leap up again, and again, which I admire –
though I know you will be bound to say
how neither the dying back nor the splendid

rising from the dry wood is more
than merely the dumb way of things;
which I, bound long in orders of Desire,

will say I have understood.

FOOTE BROOK

At the foot of the slope down which
we faltered, the night roared, the brook
being in full spate. Unbalancing,
we leaned into pliancies of birch,

caught ourselves against
pitchy hemlocks. Then,
before we had expected it,
we breathed spray –

we were almost there. Because the moon
had excited to light the edge of a cloud,
the brook at the falls leaped for an instant
with radiance – though elsewhere

light did not abound, nor could we
at that moment have said
night had by ordinary canon come
upon us. The brook was no more

than a minor brightness, yet its voice
was a powerful spasm of the night,
and the large world everywhere
so bountiful an irregularity of surfaces,

we could scarcely keep our feet.

SUNRISE

Throughout the night the sky
had been wild with stars.
Then in the morning came an instant
when the hills sharpened, and grew shadowless,

and the world seemed no casual
enterprise of creation. From beyond the hills
rose the soft pillars of light,
until, as if caught by high winds,

they wove and interwove, and became
the bright, close fabric of sky.
Later came a burst of warm rain,
but by sunset the light had cleared,

and at the tip of one needle of the white pine
that shaded the porch, a drop of rainwater
trembled. It was clear
as ice. It contained a fierce,

quivering image of the sun.
The light drew back, and back,
and with no further evidence of breath
the sky was precisely as it had ever been.

GOLDFINCH

After the goldfinch
had in a spark of panic flown,
the stalk of timothy went on
shivering. Overnight had come wind,

and the world had given way
by half, at least – the trees
nearly bare, the woods admitting
good measure of light.

As for the goldfinch,
nothing remained
except its small impulse
lent the grass, sustained

far longer than one,
moved to consider
so small an evidence
of breath, might rightly

have expected.

ORCHARD

By late afternoon the light
had given way, and the air
cooled. Mists welled
from the warm ditches,

spilled over, and merged.
We drove through the topmost layers
of a growing cloud.
From the doorsills up our house

greeted us, though directly enough
we found the steps and walked
sure-footed in, the rooms
settling a little as we entered –

this after a gilt September day
in celebration of itself
spent picking apples
in the Early Transparent orchard,

the air beneath the young trees
a dust of green light, the apples
a fragrant windfall,
so wherever we looked

there seemed to have occurred
in the grass among the strict
rows an exuberant error
of season, a great yield

of sudden yellow flowers.

The Marshes at Suamico, Wisconsin

At the edge of the marshes the cattails leaped with frogs.
One of us found twined on a sedge twig a tiny green snake,
a vigor of grassy light burning its slow way out,
picked it up, let it coil in his palm,
wave its head, flick its coral tongue –

carried it so for awhile until it grew frightened,
tensed, and gave off for so small a thing
a remarkable high-flavored reek. He flung it away,
and none of us ever could find it again, or another like it,
though we kept on the lookout. Then, deeper,

the marsh smell began, the air clean enough
till we stirred up the mud, slogging through
to the blinds, our trails filling in with a fetid
thickness of oozes, only the pale
swath of bent reeds to show how we'd come.

The lake leached in from beneath; where we walked
was something less earth than water, swelling
with bubbles that burst through the duckweed and cress,
our faces at intervals swept with clean, stony gusts
from the open lake. The mallows were springy

with redwings. Everywhere flashed the green bolts
of dragonflies; snakes and turtles cruised
the channels; feathers of mud braided lakeward. At dawn
came the ducks, the sky awash to the feathery roots
of its undersoils: flocks of mallard and canvasback,

teal that swung in over the blind, or flared
on some sheen of the wind. In the marshes at Suamico,
watchful, we felt the world borne down
by its own abundancies. Wherever we broke
through the pursy earth, there billowed about us a quick

exhalation of soils, a rich, recognizable stink,
while over us there in the dawn shone the bird-ridden sky.

CLEARING

One day together walking
careless beneath the refractive canopy
of the October woods,
we were stopped, hurled back

by solid light, our minds,
unready, flung
to the clearing's farther edge.
There we turned,

looked back to see
across a barren of ferns
our empty bodies, lost,
bewildered, sick with ignorance

and fear – but light
had intervened. Up
from the saturate heart of the earth
it sprang and flooded,

rose sulfurous in the living woods.
Everywhere about us bled
the raw, seasonal edges.
There we stood.

Fixing the Furnace

I had been no more
than repairing my old furnace
which was inconstant, and would not,

when most I required it, burn;
for I had anticipated frost,
though the season was yet summery.

And having turned one bolt and pressed
the reset, I lurched back
as without warning the furnace

startled into life,
and by God and uncommon grace –
for I had with ignorance

and the wrong tools approached
the task – from the spy hole
dazzled forth, and white with fire!

MIST

This morning some scarlet maples on the hill
were muted to pink by a mist,
and by that masking of color and the warm air
I was put next to tears,

for which I was unprepared,
being by fall beyond all other seasons
made quick and joyous to note how the blushed
yellows most enlivened the delicate woods,

that the reds and oranges close up
were fragile, dry and brown,
how among the marigolds a foot
above the ground, the frost

had touched and killed, while close
at their roots the earth was warm,
loose-soiled, as summer long.

THE ASH GROVE IN OCTOBER

October has always seemed
an error of time – who will not argue
that in this place it is the freshest
of the seasons, the loveliest, most

to be loved? Yet in one night
the ash grove deposits its leaves
in a litter of gold about
the grey boles, which sight

startles, this failure of leaves, the perennial
astonishment – though I should know,
and well enough by now,
there is nothing about the ash tree moderate,

gradual, or considered, as with the maple;
or obstinate, as with the oak.
I have learned to expect
that around the middle of October

will occur in a sudden night
the storming of leaves.
This year I see it again in the way
I have never understood,

as if the given day
were to be the last on which
I might perceive such a thing
as the unlit brilliance of ash leaves.

Not for the first time
the sight has reminded me
of something I have been unable to name,
have seen only dimly, and on occasion

during the time of the failure of leaves,
when it still seems possible
that winter will not come
and the warm hazes of October will lie

forever in great, breatheable fields
about the open-windowed houses
of our neighborhood; in which
it still seems possible

that in a single night the leaves
might burst up from the grass
like a flushed covey of small yellow birds,
and rearrange themselves on the branches,

so that in the morning we would find
our lawns to be shaded again,
yet a brightness beneath
the reawakened, light-feeding trees.

CARDINALS IN THE ICE AGE

When Louise called to tell me
that a pair of cardinals was at her feeder
and had been around for days,
I was, besides envious, reassured,

not having at my own tray seen
a cardinal in years. I had grown in fact
to fear I might not soon again.
I had thought they must have fled

the growing inclemencies of this place
to somewhere farther south, and it was clear
I had not the strategies to lure them north
again. To me this was in the way of a most

considerable loss. But here were cardinals,
or at least word of them, and any time I chose
I might cross the road and see them for myself;
and yet stayed home, for while it was a short walk,

the day was cold, the road a difficult course
of icy ruts, and they were not my cardinals,
but hers. Besides, was it not enough to know
the birds were back, there in my neighbor's yard,

bright on the vivid snow? I took this
to be rare and necessary evidence that still
some time remained before the first lobes
of the great oncoming ice on its long probe south

awakened the neighborhood one night
to the sounds of our mountains going down,
screech of rock on bedrock, huge
morainal wave of houses, trees, and boulders,

and finally the dull moon reflected
from the still face of the ice cliff
looming two miles overhead
into a birdless sky.

SNOWY OWL

One day, stopping at the barn, we looked
and simply he was gone, and has not
to the common day of any of ten winters
journeyed back. We recollect

how everywhere about the barn the world
had grown wary, quieted, and hid. But never
did we see him fly or hunt. Never
did his lonely and terrific voice augment

the neighborhood. Though overhead
had squawked and stormed a fury of crows,
he did not move or blink,
but governed there, unflawed in stillness,

except once briefly clashed
the blue hook of his beak. Oh, we
admired that wonder! but he left,
being not indigenous, and starving.

Barking Dog

From down the road and near the landlord's house
his terrible dog, whose fierce and guardian voice
kept us all close upon our boundaries,
warmed up with a few preliminary snarls,

then barked, savage, incurious, and untiring
the whole night: two sharp yelps, a pause,
and then unvarying two more – nor could I sleep.
Therefore, though I disliked at night

to walk through my over-dark and speechless house
where I must pass a room in which lurked
some uncommon terror that once
had come to someone who lived in my house

there in that room, and died; and then to walk
along the cold, light-feeding road;
nevertheless I ventured out
into the dog-voiced night, angry to be afraid,

when just at the corner of our properties
the world fell silent, and a great black dog
charged across the yard. He was silent,
he seemed not tentative, he carried

his head low. Of all the dread forms,
most I dreaded that! Slowly I backed away
afraid to turn, our eyes on one another's, till
I thought I might be safe, and flung about and ran.

Thank God he did not follow, only
all night ranged the bench marks of our yards
and barked, and barked. This happened long ago
when I was wary of malice, large and small,

convinced, though nothing could I see, that I was seen,
and had not journeyed far in understanding
whichever way I turned was always something
at my back. How was it they who lived

along the landlord's road and in his house
had borne it that long while, that voice
which overwhelmed the world,
strict of measure and extensive of dominion,

and they lived nearer than ever I lived? *Thus
in the large world peace has not yet visited!*
For his voice which troubled me was strong and large,
and carried far, and nothing drowned it out;

for so was set his measure in my head.

Unfocusing on Window,
Tree, and Sky

At first the amethyst vase, then
the screens and moldings blurred.
Dust flecks flared on the window
and dimmed, upon which entered into view

the branches of the black locust
sharp across the drive, the fabric
of leaves and limbs coiled
around burls of light. Next,

darkness against light, then blackness
against color, height, shape of crown, bulk
and density of bole. In early June
appeared the delicate, paired leaves

like fern fronds, then from the long
trailers of white blossoms
a ponderous, streaming scent
gone visible. Later, the flowers became

dry pods. Thorns sprang
in rosettes from every
crotch and joining of branch
and bole. In one of those odd and idle

gestures of reconciliation
I have accustomed myself to make
toward the world I have through God's disfavor
lost, hoping to justify it

in the fullness and perfection
of a single word, I have proposed to myself
the locust tree against the sky,
its thorny branches enclosing light,

to be a figure of loss. Over the years
often and unaccountably I have become
aware of myself moved to forlornness
and have seen it is because

without considering,
with no preparation at all,
I have found the locust sharp in my eye,
so that to spare myself

I have unfocused, and in time
the tree has receded, appeared as if it were
some element of sky, turgid
pattern of cloud or constellate

lightlessness. Just now
I have postured to a friend,
saying how it is (gesturing at the tree)
that I cannot with certainty name

nor even wholly acknowledge what I see.
But she has gone,
and holding at shorter and more proper focus
I add the event to the list of those

that this week at the oddest of times –
while peeling an orange, opening
a car door, walking across the highway
for the mail – have moved me

to a nearness of tears,
to speak out of something
like the surfacing of conviction,
to say aloud, *there will not*

after all be time
enough! and having said this
nevertheless begun quite helplessly
to refashion the image of the locust,

once more to charter the light
into starry islands between its limbs;
to draw it back into clear shape
from the deep, retentive sky.

                              —*For Ellen Lovell*

CARDINALS

I

I saw the cardinal
from the kitchen window
on one of the first warm days:
a scarlet puff at the center

of the holly bush, a red,
beaked, and black-eyed berry.
His crest lifted
to the wind. I tapped the glass,

but it was only when I walked out
and reached into the bush
so that I was no more
than five inches from taking him

into the circle of my thumb and finger
where I thought he might burn
like a small, beating flame,
that suddenly he sleeked

and flickered low across the yard
into the heart of a dark cedar.

2

The lawns were full
of green light. There was
a scarlet litter
of windfall holly berries.

Five feeding cardinals
bloomed in the grass. It was
a day for the felling of trees,
the butchering of animals,

the capture of great fish.
But I looked into the cold
blue iris of the sky,
I saw that although

I had been set upright,
I would be permitted
to fall back.

Avocados

Into the serene leaves
of the last tree of the last orchard
in La Habra, I looked up, trying to spot
avocados. I tried

a dozen angles, lay on my back,
looked over my shoulder to one side,
and then slightly to the other, stared
between my fingers, until

from the vantage of some
unplanned stance, there they were,
dozens of them, dark, pendulous,
rotten-ripe where they had hung

for days before I took it in my head
to look for them. I brought out
the long-handled snips and cut,
trying to catch them as they fell,

a couple ending in green, oily smears
in my palm. I cut them, cautious,
careful of angles, there in the green
deep shade beneath the tree,

only a yard away the parking lot
a flat of dry light, but the avocados
precisely the color of the leaves'
undersides, ready to draw back

on the inmost darkness
of the inmost seed.

TRAVELING

Afraid, I was always afraid:
we would be late, our seats
stolen, that once aboard

in the close compartments
someone would light up, and then
should I object, in anger

and contempt he would rebuke me,
on hot days require the windows
be closed, play music

too loud, pretend
not to understand when I enquired
where we might be, how far

we might have come, where we were bound,
had yet to go. That ours
might be the wrong train

through inattention
wrongly boarded, and we were lost
irretrievable, unticketed; that we

had long passed and repassed
our destination, that the intolerable
delays on the dark sidings

required firm looking into, though
to whom I ought to have addressed myself
according to what tone and stance

Derailment

Though five cars of the morning train
to Subotica careened into the river
and a man was drowned, a woman torn in two,
it happened too far from where I slept

for me to have heard . . . nonetheless
I started awake, crossed to the window,
and looked out to see the road asteam
in the warm morning, a brown wash

streaming in the ditches. Lights flashed
at the crossing, and kept on. But what
had waked me? The room
was still, I had all night

most calmly slept, no more
than ordinarily stirred, though it is true
that in my sleep I had thought myself
aware of a sky enormously thundering

and the world to its mountainous rimstones
in paroxysms of fire, and from this
had been moved to wake (to a cry,
to a rolling of thunder?), shaken

I did not know, and so continued
restless, weary, and impatient;
that there had slipped my mind

that which I from the very first
had been cautious to remember; that outside
were truly nothing but dull fields, smoke,

black snow; that it was certain we
had been rerouted, given
no notice, would not arrive,

and should have, hours ago.

to a power of unease as if myself
caught and rent in the first instant
of casual dismemberment, not yet
awake, terrified and aware

that for the usual generous brightening
of the world, for my ordinary commitment
to its authoritative light,
I had waited overlong.

SLOVENJ GRADEC

That close to the mountain
at that time of year
the frost came early.
Any who cared to look

could see how close at hand
it had all along
been gathering. The mountains
rose luminous as clouds

above the gibberish color
of the October woods.
In fact, there were no clouds,
but something intervened

for the light did not
make shadows. The planet
had long been cooling.
Already it was beyond comfort.

—for Alenka Rainer

IN BOHINJ

We stood together on the lakeshore.
The water was slow with cold.
It bloomed in soft storms of mist
that rose and joined and dazzled

around us everywhere.
We saw flung out over the lake
the streaming plumes of the mountain.
There was behind it all, we knew,

some cold power of the sun.
The sky froze and unfroze
its green veils – yet neither of us
was persuaded of the cold,

for the sky engendered a light
by which from the beginning
had we thought to look
we might plainly have beheld the world.

The Hunters

Traveling, our plans in ruin
by reason of the unseasonable snow,
the day gone sour with the silences we kept,
through the dark afternoon impatient

for the Belgrade train, we waited
in the bitter restaurant
of the Vojvodina Hotel,
of our poor and cold room dispossessed

to favor the Italian hunters who complained
one table away about the dogs, their guides,
our room, the moldy bread, a cup
with a chipped lip . . . or so Miša in scorn

translated for us, saying it was "*normal*," this
was the way in this place at this hotel
at this time of the year, anyone
ought to have expected it to be.

But we had not so expected it to be,
for oh, but the yellow grease congealed
on the chill, unhappy restaurant plates,
upstairs sat empty our room we could not use,

and all the while far out on the foggy plain
pheasants preened and crowed and crowded
in the stubbles of the maize fields, hares
played in multitudes beyond imagining,

roebuck bellowed and leaped at the forest's edge
in herds, in herds! Everywhere browsed and rooted
fallow deer and boar, the marshes were raucous
with geese, big pike and carp threshed

the shallows into foam. Had we
the inclination, we could fish and hunt.
But we were cold and tired,
and we yearned for sleep; besides,

against the windows rained a slush
of snow and fog and coal smoke; our weapons
lay disassembled in their sleeves; and whatever
remained of the light, it did not count.

—for Mira and Miša Stanić

Chestnuts

Nothing so imprisoned the young light
of the fall afternoon, or with such urgency
returned it, as the ripe chestnuts
by the river wind shaken from the trees

to scatter lustrous in the grass,
in the beds of winter roses. They rained
onto the parked cars all day along
Lovdenska Ulica, exploded

on the boulevards, and we dodged
and covered our heads against
the bounty of dangerous sweet chestnuts
in October, in Novi Sad.

TAXI

From over our driver's shoulder
in the rear-view mirror I observed
the angry driver of the scarlet Zastava
with both hands rend his head and lean

raging into the windshield. Traffic was hot
and solid to either side, and close
the red car followed, swerving
and desperate to pass. Our driver, loud

in his power, sang joyful to the radio,
and I – I huddled, certain we would die,
and begged to slow him down, but lacked
syntax; so there we were,

hurtling terrified along
the very center line
of Marsala Tita, and God knew
what lay ahead. Once I thought

to leap the seat and wrest the wheel away,
but saw that then we were the more inevitably
doomed, being travelers, strangers, lost
and insufficient, unable

with clarity to see enough ahead
to mark our proper turnings
and prepare for them.

HOMESICK

Never before had we seen leaves
shrivel on the very trees, apples
harden and fall before they were ripe.
But at last, after five months

without rain, it rained. Streams thickened
with mud and scoured
the valleys, and what remained
of the village gardens vaguely greened.

In the bus terminal at Skopje,
because the floor was tracked
with a grease of clayey mud,
a woman from Bitola skidded, and falling,

scattered a hundred paprikas,
citron, red, lime-gold and green.
Helping her gather these up, I was brought
to think of the garden I had left behind

in order that I might discover myself to be
precisely where that moment I knelt
scrambling for her spilled fruit. I thought
of pepper plants in the cool mornings, flowering

melons and pumpkins, carrots
bulging the soil. I did not doubt
that care would not have been taken
in my absence; therefore also that

all must by now have yielded
to a wilderness of moonflowers
and bindweed, the onions
maggoty, the eggplants

fallen nightly one by one, soft
in the soft mulch. None of it
could I confirm, for I was traveling, and far.
But there, from the smeared floor,

from beneath benches, from out
of the thickets of shadow, from among
the careless boots of strangers
retrieving bright peppers, I considered

the orders of husbandry, rubbed
one yellow fruit against my cheek,
thought somewhere in the dank corners
of the windowless and evil-smelling room

might yet reside fair evidence
of the love and wrath
of the creation; went
on looking; longed for home.

Ohrid

Within the month we had swum
at a green height in the warm lake,
while only yesterday,
black and ashy to the knees,

we'd bushwhacked the burnt slopes,
come down to the groves
where bees clustered at the jellied masses
of almond sap, and the earth was sticky

with windfall figs . . . whereupon
arrived an unseasonable cold, so bitter
that the sour watchman in the orchard
would not suffer himself to unpocket

his hands, not even to brandish
his rifle when he surprised us
looting there. Lizards clung to the tiles
and fell. Against all advice and reason

we had come, too late in the year. What
had made us consider we might be
exempt? Only that each night
in the final days before the cold,

the lower the sun had fallen
on the horizon, the brighter
the lake had shone.

THE RECOGNITION

Before the photograph of the hostages
milling in the snowy yard I lingered
until the guide called out,

and could not for my life
think who might have been the one
listless in the middle rank,

propping himself against the pocked wall,
featureless, white-shirted, bald,
among them all he so stood out to me.

In the Revolutionary
Museum at Ljubljana

Row on row of double photographs, before-
and-after, images so direct
as to invite study before horror,
a dozen or so hostages (some women

in aprons, an old man scratching
his thigh), all fairly
casual, for perhaps
it was the first occasion, and none of them

chose to know what it was all
about, or did not understand
the protocol, or figured it
for a bluff, or simply

went on thinking about the taste
of bread still in the backs
of their mouths, the smell
of cooking fires, autumn leaves

everywhere drifting. Crowns
of big chestnuts flowered
in the background. Dogs
yawned beneath wagons, children

clambered on the walls. But then,
in the interval, some huge
and unrecorded violence would have taken place,
and next they would all be lying

as in the throes of a terrible dream,
legs and arms wracked
askew, heads flung
back, wrenched sideways, every

one of them with their mouths
sprung wide. The children
would have vanished, and the dogs
would be looking at the camera, friendly

and attentive. I had to take on faith
the trees were ripening
their fruits. It is not too much to say
I came to know everything

we know against ourselves.
But I had not expected
in horror such dispassion, seeing
how nothing followed from what I saw

because I was alive.

NIGHT CRY IN LJUBLJANA

Everywhere around us as we slept
little vacuoles of noise flickered
in the dark, small sparks
of sound, no more

than wind might make
at an edge of paper. Then from deep
in the warrens of the hotel court
they configured a single voice which rose

and wearied, rose again
and fell. It came to no regard
but mine, though pale light
which might have been reflected

from a face came through
the window. That night,
the next and next, I searched
and found among the bottle crates

and sour middens of cabbage leaves
nothing. I had hoped
to pick out some nameable shape
with hair and teeth and eyes

from the noisome clutter
of that yard where I feared
whatever cried lay dying, crushed
under rubbish, leg caught or collared

and strangling in a snarl
of wire – failing that,
then have it expire cleanly
into silence. But on it went, and on,

as in the exile of nightmare a voice
uneven, everywhere and unassigned,
lacking tongue, without
capacity. What cried in pain

from the dark and the rank mazes
of rubble? How was it
that ever I had forgiven myself
warmth, stupidity, anger, love, regret?

I thought that in the terrible
and very instant when it ceased,
all with it might for love and justice cease,
and the world so quiet itself

that, wary to think the cry
might any time resume itself,
we would never hear more
than the fearful silence that required it.

PICNIC

That night the sky
had brightened with a storm
no one expected; but at dawn
it grew dark. Everyone had sat

in rows on long benches in the park
at the edge of the river, the tall
grandfather, fingers thrust
through the gills of a large carp

held aloft for the photographer
to admire; the grandmother, younger
than anyone living
could possibly remember her

to have been; children, aunts; uncles
in shawls; a dog,
a pet crow on a pony's back.
But everything in that photograph

is long since dead, even the children, the dog,
the pony; even the light
clouding over the lake
and the bright grass. Patches of damp

had spread on the women's skirts.
Not a shadow was cast, and every object
shone with some manner of light.
How they assumed their lives! The brim

of the old man's hat blew back, his beard
ruffled, her skirt ballooned
a little in the wind. By now
they have forgotten the light, the river,

the occasion, each other, everything.
Had I known them
they would have forgotten me as well,
and I would have lost

even that little store of breath;
for I would have come upon them
unexpected, as they arranged themselves
on the benches by the Danube

and stiffened in the required poses,
no place in that close order, and no time
to spare a traveler, a stranger at that,
requiring direction, lost

and strangely grateful for his need,
but lacking the tongue;
and though inclined
to fail at the most familiar truth,

stubborn in the manner of travelers
to discern and name it; moreover ready
in his abominable accent
to persist.

—for Ivan Gadjansky

DEAD DOG

At the edge of everything that moved and spoke
was the smile of the dead dog
which for days had lain vividly crushed
into the coarse grain of the road.

No, this was not the first time
we had surprised ourselves coming on it,
for this was our usual way. The sea wind
buzzed in the dry beards of the palms,

the trees bent sharply inland. The air scoured
our windows with powdery sand,
though at times less voraciously,
upon which we ventured out, each time

freshly startled to come upon
such dispirit of form, lacking
the usual engagements of beauty.
We went on, though it was true that at times

we were at night afraid, standing
on the seawall, our eyes
grainy with salt. We feared
the seething space before us

from which we knew the sea
crawled blindly in,
just as we feared the face
which some nights we discovered

glaring in from the pelted darkness
outside our window, claws fanned wide
at the ears to make the figure
of the fanged and resurrectionary skull.

Oh, then we drew back against
the headboard, and held
to one another. Meanwhile, our room
emptied itself of light; meanwhile

there was backrush of light
on that discountenance.

BADLANDS

We came down into the dry bottoms,
a scorpion mangled in the knuckle
of the wiper blade, yet struggling.
At every intersection grew huddles

of fussy crosses, yellow and pink,
fretted and scrolled, garlanded
with hibiscus. We saw to the east
the shrivelled sea. West, the mountains

spilled to the sandy basins. North
was a visible heat, and over everything
spread blue, membranous dusts. But ahead
the road ran empty, except

for a crushed iguana, skull crested
and agape, straining a little
from the green, leathery shred
of its body; once, a dismembered dog;

on the windshield at eye level, at near
and particular focus, an arc
of strawy venom dried
to crystals, where the scorpion,

wind-crushed and clawless, had struck
and struck; the skeleton of a cow,
there in its belly the heaped,
incorruptible turds.

COBRA

I fear the cobra that the keeper
has teased from its box, which has reared
and spread its hood, hissed, lunged
at the keeper's yellow boots, gathered,

struck, regathered. I shudder back
from the edge of the pit, gather myself,
for though the keeper desperately has tried
to distract him, I have been singled out,

he has fixed on me, he has broken loose,
in a flash is at my feet, rising there
in the terrible display. And like no one before him
and nothing I have ever hoped to know,

he is so eagerly alert to the quick
lick of my blood that, though he does not
immediately strike, I feel spread
from the clenched heart I find I have

until this moment only indeterminately borne,
a paralysis of exaltation, a long
shiver of acknowledgment so powerful
that suddenly I have found my hand

to have extended itself, to be wavering
only inches from his open jaws,
thumb and fingers fusing into the glossy plates
of a snake's head, becoming eyed, intent, fanged,

and then lengthening into a scaled body
that unroots itself from my shoulder,
falls and coils, spreads the eyed hood,
rears, readies – so that there at my feet

I see them look back
each at the dreadful other, I see
each stare both ways
in the wary, commensurate longing.

—for Julia Alvarez

FLICKER

Spotting the road-killed flicker
on the white center line, I stopped the car
and walked back. I saw
the black crescent of his breast,

the folded wings, head broken
to one side, the red nape, a bead of blood
bright at each nostril. I picked him up
and found him limp, warm, the membranes

not yet milky on his eyes. I pinched up
the papery blue skin of the saddle,
slit it, peeled it from the bone
and bright fascia, cut off the wings, the claws,

the brown-barred cape, detached the skull
at the first cervical vertebra, and tossed away
what was left, my fingers coppery
with blood. And just then

as I cleaned my knife in the sand
beside the road, out of no instance,
out of no warning at all,
there came over me so urgent, so dizzy a swell

of longing that I with the bloody feathers
in my hand raised my hand to my face,
touched my eyes, brushed at my lips, thinking
that with the next deep undulation of pulse

my chest would tear open and my heart
fly out to roll at my feet beside
the sandy carcass of the bird.
I did not ask what I loved – only

by some fierce necessity took up
the knife and wrapped the feathers
about the bone handle and traced
the clean cutting edge along the blue

channel of a vein until my chest
was running with beads of my blood –
and I lost courage, could not
cut deeper, not knowing what it was

moved me, that I would
in time over and over,
never expecting it, leap
to the recognition.

THE SILENCE

The one child having in manner of speaking fled,
his brother ran out on the porch to call him back.
"*Philip!*" he cried out, "*Philip!*" I caught him up,
thinking if ever the dead were to be recalled

it would be in similar voice flung confident
into the raving light. Since then
each fall when the woods darken with color
the horror has been absurdly to wonder

if I in my sternest father's voice
had commanded into the bloodied gullet of the day
Come back! Come back! he might have heard.
But on the hill

the pines had strained to a power of wind.
Come back! I might have cried, but I did not,
and silence stormed. Meanwhile
he is speechless, dark, of no intent.

Patterns of Sleep

That man – photographed in sleep
by red light so that the green blanket
had gone black, and his face seemed scalded,
bedclothes tangled around his legs and spilling

onto the floor, head wired and taped
(but for all that clearly agreeable to it,
easy enough in mind to have gone to sleep
in a strange room before a camera, under

an unnatural light, likely even dreaming)
– that man without knowing it, and before
our very eyes, came close to dying: abruptly
stopped breathing, reached out without haste

one arm into the vivid light beyond the bed,
struggled up onto the other elbow, raised
his open mouth as if to drink rain, and then,
after a long time during which he was,

as we could see, calmly, motionlessly
struggling, everything resumed – first
the slow folding of his body back
onto the bed, next the breath, finally,

it may be assumed, though we
could not be sure of it, the dream –
all this, as the narrator assured us,
common enough, each of us the moment we close

our eyes at great and common risk, no matter
where we might be, nor the character
of the light, our dream
which we cannot except in rare event

remember, replaced for an instant
every night with nothing,
or with some slow upwelling
of fiery light we discover

we have all along deeply
enclosed; and then, an instant
before we awake, giving way, drawing back
into itself, leaving behind

the red stain of light
by which the camera sees,
and of which upon awakening
we remember precisely nothing,

though we feel something must have escaped us
and wonder what it might have been,
and why we are wherever
we may be, how

we could have agreed to this,
why after all these years of taking breath
and before that of breathing like a small
translucent fish the warm salines

of blood it should suddenly
seem difficult, something
about which it seems possible,
even necessary, to make a decision.

THE RAFT

His father told him
to be careful, to go no farther
than the boundaries
of the lily cove. His father

told him again about his cousin Archie
who had fallen into the scalding water
of the switchyard sump, because
the cinders floating there between the tracks

had made it seem to be
dry ground. "He wasn't thinking
where he was. He wasn't watching, he was thinking
of something else," his father said.

And he agreed he would watch
where he was going, wanting badly
to get down to the lake and out
to where he could not see

the bottom any more and where
it would not be evidently safe.
"That day he never came home
to eat, he never came home, he was dead,

and nobody knew or cared, they just
went on with whatever it was
they were doing for themselves!"
His father was going on and on

into the room like that
when he ran out the door and down
to the old dock, and found the raft
hidden in the reeds along the shore,

splintery pine boards scummy
with mud and moss; and when
he pushed it into the knee-
deep water at the end

of the dock, and stood, it ducked
and wavered and nearly
heaved him off . . . but held,
an inch awash, instep-deep.

He sprawled down onto his belly
and paddled out with his hands,
and it was like swimming –
from the house his father

looking out might have seen him
confidently swimming, buoyed
onto the surface, heading out beyond
the safe boundaries, but in fact

more safe than ever he had been
or ever might hope to be, even
should he range beyond the cove
and the dark line where the wind began –

though it was strange
to cup his hand about his eyes, lean
close to the surface of the lake
so that his nose touched water,

and look down to see, inches below,
the dense golden field of the weed.
It was strange to want so much
to stand up on the raft, step boldly off,

and walk over the feathery tips of weed
to shore, his father watching him,
walk straight on shore and call up
to the terrified house,

he is safe and has come back, and the lake
has borne him up as he had known it would,
and there had been from the very beginning
nothing to worry about, nothing at all.

Staring down into the pale water,
still bellied into the raft, he saw
the thin skin of the lake thicken
with fiery clouds, because the sky

had thickened with fiery clouds
and become opaque, so that there
as in the end, this time in the blazing lake,
in the pale cloud of his unwary face

was the awful issue of the looking back.

—for Hayden

THE PHOTOGRAPH

From the line of young birch on the far shore
crows called, erupted into the sky
out of the yellow leaves, flurried there,
fell back. The sun was high,

everything in perfect order on the raft,
the anchor rope in a tight spiral, weighed
by the red coffee can half filled
with cedar-smelling loam

from the edge of the swamp. He spilled
a handful onto the rough pine
of the deck, threaded a worm, and let it down,
careful it didn't snag, until the line

went slack, and he thought the lead
must have touched bottom, drew it up a bit,
then waited, leaning over, trying to see
into the shadows among the twists

of pickerel weed, the light
where it touched the water going green,
slanting down into the weed beds, silvery
with water dusts and pollens. Over the clean

sand bottom schools of yellow perch,
bluegills, redeyes, lavender and flash
of shiners, waver and ripple of light,
short bursts of gold and green

where the young bass fed. But nothing
happened, nothing. He waited for a fish,
and when he looked up, his eyes
dazzled at the sky. It was as if he still

were looking into the water, for the sun
was low, and a green light rose
soft from the cedars. His mother stood
on the beach and called, but he chose

not to hear, though she called and called.
At last he looked to land
and saw her farther off than he had thought,
her dress blowing, her feet in deep sand.

And so he began to paddle back, the raft
wanting to turn in circles, the wind
against him; so he stood and leaned
into the paddle, dug hard, looked up again

and saw the beach was empty, the lake
ruffling, the water going dense
and steely. It took him more time
than he'd thought he had. It was not

as if he'd truly had a choice – the wind
had turned against him, and when
he stared into the water, his face
did not stare back. He felt the rain begin,

and while he struggled toward the beach
his mother returned, and took a photograph
that caught the raft low in the slight chop,
seeming a powerful distance from shore,

and him, paddle in hand, his knickers
drooping, the birch on the far shore
bristling from snowy sand, everything
badly overexposed. It frightened him to see

how far out on the lake he had been.
He was frightened that he could not see
his face, but only a dark shape
under the hat brim. Even though

it had been in Klondike, in the general store
where he'd stood to hold and see the photograph,
under his early-summer feet the plank floor
dry and gritty, it hadn't at all

been certain that the foolish one
in the photograph was not slowly sinking
into the pale lake, endangered
and alone, calling out

to the mother who stood intent,
her camera to her eye, framing him there,
catching the birches, the crows overhead,
the lake rising on them both – somehow

even the fishy air gathering, and the sky
gathering, and around him the deepening smell
of cedar before rain, the blue surge of lightning
for an instant withheld.

—for Dave and Julie

THE SEA AT LONG POINT

In early morning from Long Point
the sea became indistinguishable
from light. By midday
it had breathed upward,

infiltrated the air,
become luminous haze.
But in the deep part of the night,
when, time having given way,

not rarely would I start awake
grieving and angry
at how it had overridden me,
there was no saying what shape the sea

might have rendered itself to be,
that outside among the rocks
chopped soft, whose breath –
heavy with sea lavender

and beach plums, rank
from the aspirate granite,
rose so thick it clouded the room.

The Planet

Through binoculars last night, my arm
braced on the porch stanchion, I saw
from Long Point over the aura of Portland
the bright disc of Jupiter, behind it

the old light of Cygnus. Brilliant,
the images wavered, yet clear at first
as otherwise and elsewhere the world
did not seem clear, nor the sky

above the world . . . two little moons
to my east of the planet, or three, the huge
discrete motions of the body
frozen there, nothing moving except

by blood tremor my hand shook so
over that time of distance that the small
trembling magnified itself, and the planet
danced, and nothing

would submit itself to focus.

COMET

In 1910 when I was eight,
mother took me from my bed and out
into the yard and pointed, and there
over our house it shone, higher

than the trees. It streamed
and billowed light, in the sky terrible
as an angel of God hovering,
about to stoop,

trailing long hair and robes
of fire. I was only eight, and felt
terrified to see that sight, and privileged,
and never have

forgotten it. None of us
on the lawn that night,
with everything else just the way
it always was – the tree frog

that sounded like a small bird dreaming
peeping away in the low crotch
of the chestnut, the drone
of crickets, across the street

somebody hunting night crawlers,
his lantern moving slow
along the edges of the flower beds,
the scarlet or yellow of a tulip

flashing out of the dark from time to time –
none of us knew how
to take it. Even today, talking it over,
we're still not sure we could have seen

a thing like that, though our minds
are clear, and we remember it
as if it were the night before. And that's
not all. Early next morning

the yard still dark, from the holly bush
a cardinal was singing, and from
the hickory, a mockingbird,
and for a minute there, not quite

over the line to wakefulness
and probably by what I'd seen
still blinded to the usual ways of things,
I thought the trees

were singing. In my long life
have not been many times like that one, first
a huge firework in the heaven, a slow explosion
that stayed alight, then trees

singing. But soon enough
I was awake, and knew better,
and for years
have known better. For years, till now,

the comet has held
the other recollection down.
I don't know why
it comes back to me at all,

for of that night I can't recall
anything of any person there,
not even of my mother, who held me
and spoke low, not how

she looked, or what
her voice was like, her words,
it was so long ago. Probably
I used the dream of trees

to balance off the terror
I must have felt, being only eight . . .
the wonder of it, allowed up late
beyond late in the face

of all that light. The trees sang
as if the world had taken in
and changed and was returning
whatever sweetness might have lain

buried at the heart of all that fire.
Though it was the smaller event,
by far, it burns
powerful in my memory as the sight

of that thing in the sky.
I'll take it to the grave,
though I don't know why
I should remember it at all,

for that trees might sing
had seemed, in the face of so wild
a presence, no equal wonder,
had borne with it nothing of terror

or disbelief; and surely
there must be things I ought
from duty of love better
to have remembered for being

dearer to me, and yet
are lost, gone out and lost
forever, and forever
have not sung back to me.

WINTER FLIGHT

I

Just now, here on the runway at Milwaukee,
already three hours late into Ontario
by way of Denver, which is filled
beyond all possibility with snow,

my invalid father, who has always feared
to fly, comes back just long enough
to ask me, who is shepherding him west,
are we airborne? an hour yet from taking off,

and he, the whole time here beside me
so far as I can tell, half-dead,
mouth agape, a dark stain down
one trouser leg, eyes rolled into his head,

asking so as to display some shape
of interest, staring out the window
into the garish nightmare of blue runway lights
each in its pool of blue snow, that snow-

flood in a cold place neither of us
is likely to see again, nor cares to see;
then, sagging back into his seat on the dead
leg, dead arm, sour smell of the old meat

giving way, asks *how high are we?*
goes still, tries himself once hard to shove
himself upright, and fails. And I cannot help or speak
for being one who, wishing to move, moves.

2

In the thrust and vigorous angle
of the aircraft when at last
it rises, and we enter the black sky
of winter that arcs from here and west

and east of here to as far as we might
in order of safety wish to go – when
at last it rises, piercing the night clouds,
entering the watery currents of the high wind,

it is as he has been promised he should fear:
earth-pull as he could never have
imagined it, stony masses of the continent,
power of water calling after him come back!

flesh of belly, breasts and balls
hauled at, even the smallest
of his small bloods hauled at,
and in tumult to the east and west

the great seas he has never seen
about to spill out over the cold land,
below him the angry shallows of the lakes,
below him the forests of Wisconsin

lashing away, and ahead the mountains
sharply in wait, rising and hardening, ahead
and beneath him nothing with much
in the way of promise to it. Half-dead

he is for the first time flying,
and the last, over the calm flowering
of the moonlit clouds, torn loose
from the entire beloved matter of things,

moving himself to move, fearing it is
in any but the most formal of descents
nothing but annihilation, flesh strewn
about the icy fields of the blue-lit planet,

which, as it turns out, falls away,
thrusts up, billows with snow and salt, surges
together, calls after him, boils up
at its ravenous verges.

Two Days

In the Metro station from the foot
of the dead escalator, uncertain I looked
five stories up into the eye of daylight
and wondered did I dare to climb those stairs?

But tried, hoping to outlast my body, which
in recent years had not precisely raged
against me, yet had come
precisely not to love me. Then

something intervened between the light and me.
That part of myself that wished to breathe and see
did not with grace respond, and in my breast
raw shadow unshaped itself, and tore away.

Abruptly I emerged into the wintry day
coughing and blinking, gasping for air and light,
and on the pavement at my feet rolled bright
a dozen yellow apples, one

crushed into white pulp turning brown,
together with a scatter of bronze mums.
It was cold, and nothing moved. Beneath
the pavement stirred the coiled world.

The sun illuminated as from within
the yellow apples. The flowers dully flamed.
Thus was lovely and composed the day
wherein resumed its light. Therefore

I was casual with Zimmer, and I said
that by all the evidence I might soon die.
But he condemned the thought. Thereafter
it was never more than simple favor to a friend

I loved, neither to die nor further speak of it.
But one day later, driving north through fog,
with little trust I safely would arrive,
I saw some fool of sounder heart stop dead

in the southbound lane to read his map.
And frequently I was passed by drivers
free and joyous in their cars. But I
had grown timid for having seen

deformed in me the voluntary and intentional –
with hours to go I felt not in control:
how readily my car might slide
into the ditch, and trap me there

where helpless I would die, remembering
how only one day before a light
of which I had been unaware
abruptly had gone out, and I,

astounded by pain, had slumped
against the wall, and felt
the backthrust of the lively soils beyond.
But though I lacked the strength to raise my arms

and to either side reach out and touch the stone
and could not therefore join to myself
that power, at least I did not fall.
I might have thought,

what is diminished here? how long
before no light remains to be used up?
but had seen instead that in my need
I was not to be forsaken by the massive world

which theretofore I called unyielding.
For the care I felt, the steering wheel
leaped lively in my hand. The driver
close upon me following grew wary, likewise

who followed him. We were alive.
It had been from the very first that close a thing.
Speeding along just south of Albany,
into the orotund, whole-hearted weathers

of the north, oh we were but a whisker from
annihilation, and we knew it! Shrubs of fog
bloomed wild in the right-of-way. And yet
perhaps not wholly out of reach

did Exit 13 offer fuel and food,
while at 14 was maybe lodging to be had.

—for Paul

Revisit

The clear disk of the sun
was dim on the horizon as the moon.
I could by its light discern
less than prospect, for nothing

described itself except
it was rendered out of loss
or loneliness. In my tracks
the snow smoked and swirled

as if fire were on the verge
of breaking through.
Light had begun to penetrate
the ice on the windows,

to drift over the floors,
climb slantingly the walls.
I imagined how in late afternoon
it might free itself once more

to the bitter yard
from which I should by then
have for hours been gone –
though for the moment light sustained

the deep, familiar rubbles
of emptiness. In the wintry yard
I stood to reclaim right
of property, and looked

up at the windows, one of which
I recalled to have opened
onto the fragrance
of the lavender lilac, the other

onto that of the white.

TEXT AND COVER DESIGN BY TREE SWENSON

COVER ARTIST IS MARY GRIEP

TEXT TYPE IS JANSON

TYPE SET BY WILSTED & TAYLOR

MANUFACTURED BY ARCATA GRAPHICS